# LEGO CITY

# Busy Word Book

Written by
**Joseph Stewart**

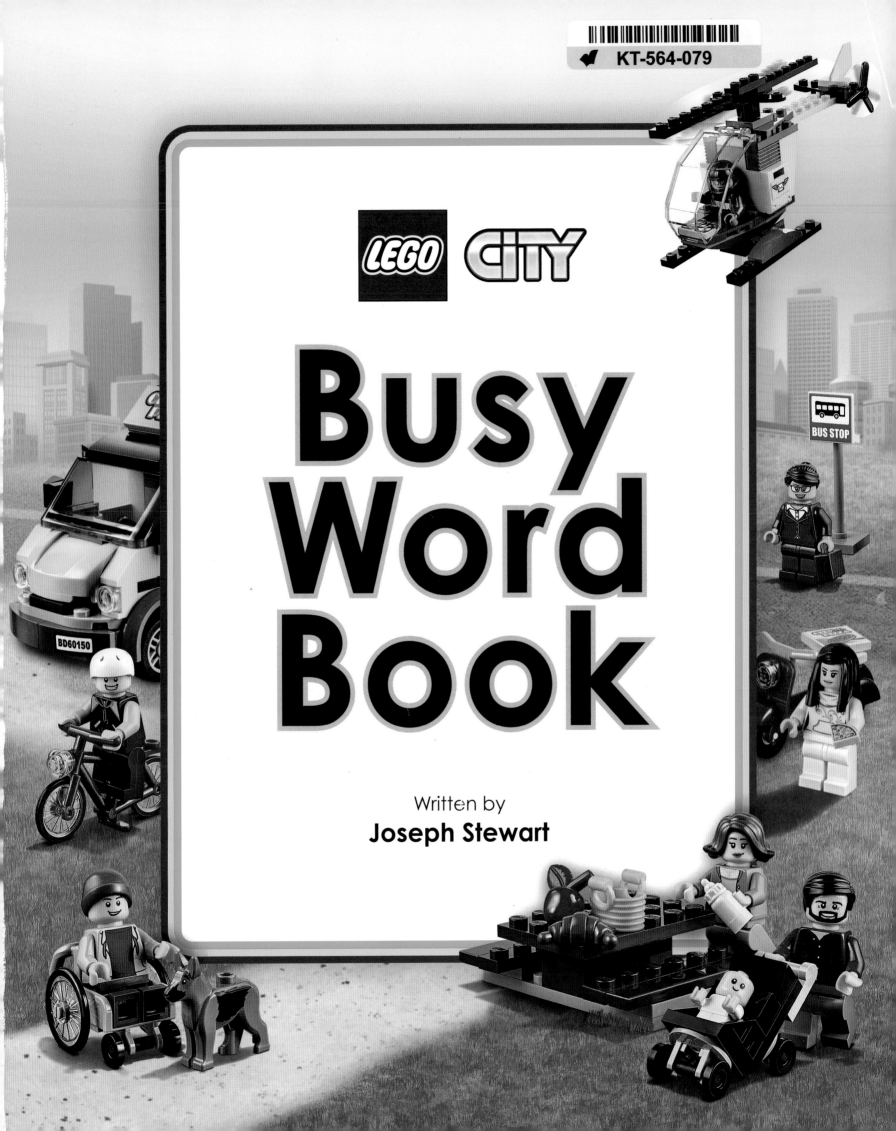

BUS STOP

# Contents

There are three small objects to find in each scene. Look out for the "Can you find?" feature. Try and spot them all!

Can you find?

a spider

a radio

flowers

# CHAPTER ONE

# In the City

There is lots to do in LEGO® City. People shop in the city centre. People relax on the beach and play in the park. Workers help to keep LEGO City on the move. Let's go and visit!

businesswoman

brake lights

door

bumper

There's a crook on the loose.
Look out for him in every scene!

# A busy day in LEGO® City

It is always busy in LEGO City. People wait to board the tram. A news helicopter flies above the city. A crook is running through the crowd. He has stolen a tasty pizza!

I'm on the lookout for a hungry crook! Can you spot him?

flag

car

service centre

recovery vehicle

Stop that pizza crook!

hot-dog cart

pizza delivery bike

dog

conductor

bicycle carriage

tram

Can you find?

a sausage

a yellow mug

a pretzel

shop window

news helicopter

toy shop

car lift

delivery lorry

delivery man

I'll be back for a sausage!

crates

zebra crossing

tram station

bicycle

coffee shop

newspapers

7

# Playing in the park

LEGO City park is a great outdoor place to go. Two children play a game of football on the green grass. A family enjoys a picnic. The fence is being repainted.

pizza van

parasol

I've heard there is a crook on the loose!

helmet

hot dog

cyclist

Good boy!

tongs

twins

grandfather

dog

playground roundabout

wheelchair

BD60150

# A new neighbourhood

The new town square is nearly finished. A crane lowers a big stone statue. A skateboarder rolls past the bus stop. The chef is giving out free pizza today!

parasol

A little to the right...perfect!

crane

statue

barrier

chef

plinth

crane operator

bus driver

Can you find?

a newspaper

City Financial News

a pizza

a radio

# At the beach

LEGO City beach is always busy on a sunny day. Some people play volleyball and build sandcastles. Others relax in the shade. A dolphin dives high out of the water!

Can you find?

a bucket

a fish

a parrot

boom box

hammock

ice cream

The beach is my favourite place!

customers

ice-cream seller

paddle

kayak

dolphin

diver

# Minifigures at work

Special vehicles are used to keep LEGO City clean and tidy. The bin lorry empties the skip. The street sweeper brushes dirt from the roads. The digger picks up rubble and rocks.

bin lorry

cab

loading arm

recycling symbol

rearview mirror

skip

Can you find?

a banana

a hazard light

money

overalls

traffic cones

rubbish

# Minifigures at work

Special vehicles are used to keep LEGO City clean and tidy. The bin lorry empties the skip. The street sweeper brushes dirt from the roads. The digger picks up rubble and rocks.

bin lorry

cab

loading arm

recycling symbol

rearview mirror

skip

Can you find?

a banana

a hazard light

overalls

money

traffic cones

rubbish

Can you find?

a rat

an ice cream

a cat

wrecking ball

boom

giant crane

door

hard hat

winch

10 T

crane operator

Easy does it... oops!

detonator handle

caterpillar tracks

STOP

17

# Express delivery

Welcome to the LEGO City cargo terminal! The crane loads containers onto the lorry trailer. When the lorry is ready to go, the guard will raise the barrier and let it pass.

storage unit

lorry

kiosk

guard

cargo

I don't know, but he sounds hungry!

barrier

Who is this crook everyone is talking about?

sack truck

lights

forklift

pallet

container

crane

folding door

trailer

lorry cab

gas cylinders

car transporter

struts

clipboard

Can you find?

a briefcase

a radio

a snake

businessman

car

19

# CHAPTER TWO

# Emergency!

It takes a brave team of police, firefighters, coast guards and doctors to keep LEGO® City safe! Whenever someone is in trouble, they are the first on the scene. There is no emergency they can't handle.

fire engine

firefighter

HA60110

sirens

Remember to look out for the pizza crook!

# Keeping LEGO® City safe

Emergency at the LEGO City police station! Two crafty crooks are trying to help their friend escape prison. Luckily the police don't have to travel very far to solve this crime.

satellite dish

All officers look out for the pizza crook!

control tower

stairs

radio

garage

POLICE

police motorbike

Can you find?

a crowbar

handcuffs

a monkey

POLICE

police car

# Double trouble

The LEGO City police are very busy tonight. They have heard reports of two burglaries. The burglaries are right next door to each other! The police arrive quickly at the scene to stop the crooks.

Hey, don't leave me behind!

bank

safe

chain

alarm

security camera

bulldozer

ATM

police dog

Can you find?

a banana

a statue

a frog

police van

zebra crossing

police officer

# Crooks' hideout

Crooks hide from the police in a swamp just outside the city. They live in a rickety shack on a dock. The police have found them. A chase across the swamp begins!

metal roof

safe

handcuffs

vines

snake

dinghy

Full speed ahead!

Can you find?

a chicken leg

a plunger

a guitar

hovercraft

swamp

windmill

chimney

spider

Watch out for alligators, Chief!

floats

window

alligator

dock

police chief

off-road vehicle

CG60068

radio

mini hovercraft

# Police at the ready

The LEGO City police have lots of special equipment to help them fight crime. No crook is safe from their speedy vehicles, high-tech equipment and clever police dogs!

horns

radar

police officer

headphones

grill

bone

winch

tyre

Good boy!

police dog

traffic cone

AC60139

aerial

folding doors

cell

computer

truck

dog van

Hmm, that's strange! I can smell pizza!

handcuffs

HS60048

POLICE

POLICE

siren

POLICE

buggy

Can you find?

money

a radio

a wrench

29

# Firefighters: go, go, go!

LEGO City fire department is always ready to respond to emergencies. The alarm rings and the firefighters spring into action. One slides all the way down the fireman's pole!

helmet

This is making my head spin!

radar

fireman's pole

fire car

equipment

Fire! Fire! Save my cart!

oxygen tank

dalmatian

hot-dog vendor

hot-dog cart

nozzle

Can you find?

an alarm
an axe
a gold helmet

fire helicopter

water tank

bunkbeds

helipad

garage

entrance

lifting arm

Save me a hot dog!

fire chief

firefighter

stabilisers

fire hose

60110

HA60110

# Call the coast guard

Oh dear! A boat and its crew are in danger. The LEGO City coast guard are on their way. They will rescue the crew. Watch out for sharks!

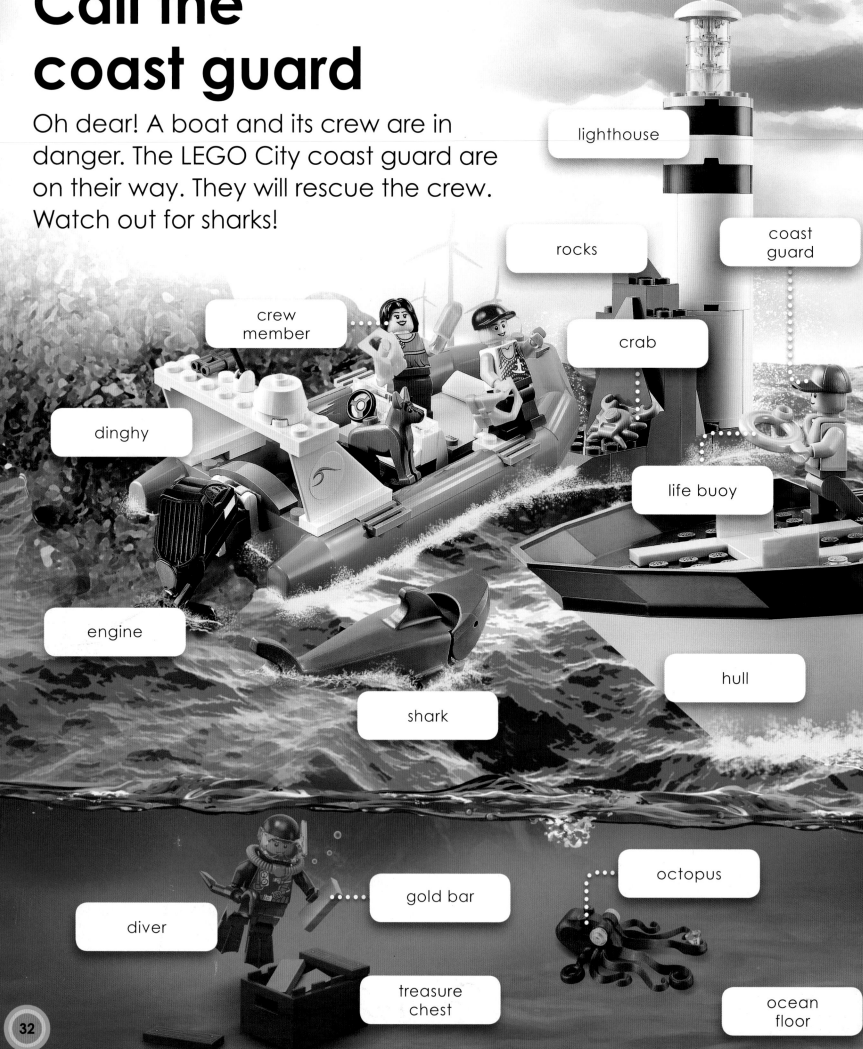

lighthouse

rocks

coast guard

crew member

crab

dinghy

life buoy

engine

hull

shark

octopus

diver

gold bar

treasure chest

ocean floor

# Helicopter hospital

Oh no! Someone has slipped on a banana peel outside the hospital. The paramedic arrives in the ambulance to help him. The helicopter flies off to another emergency. Patients feel better in no time at LEGO City Hospital.

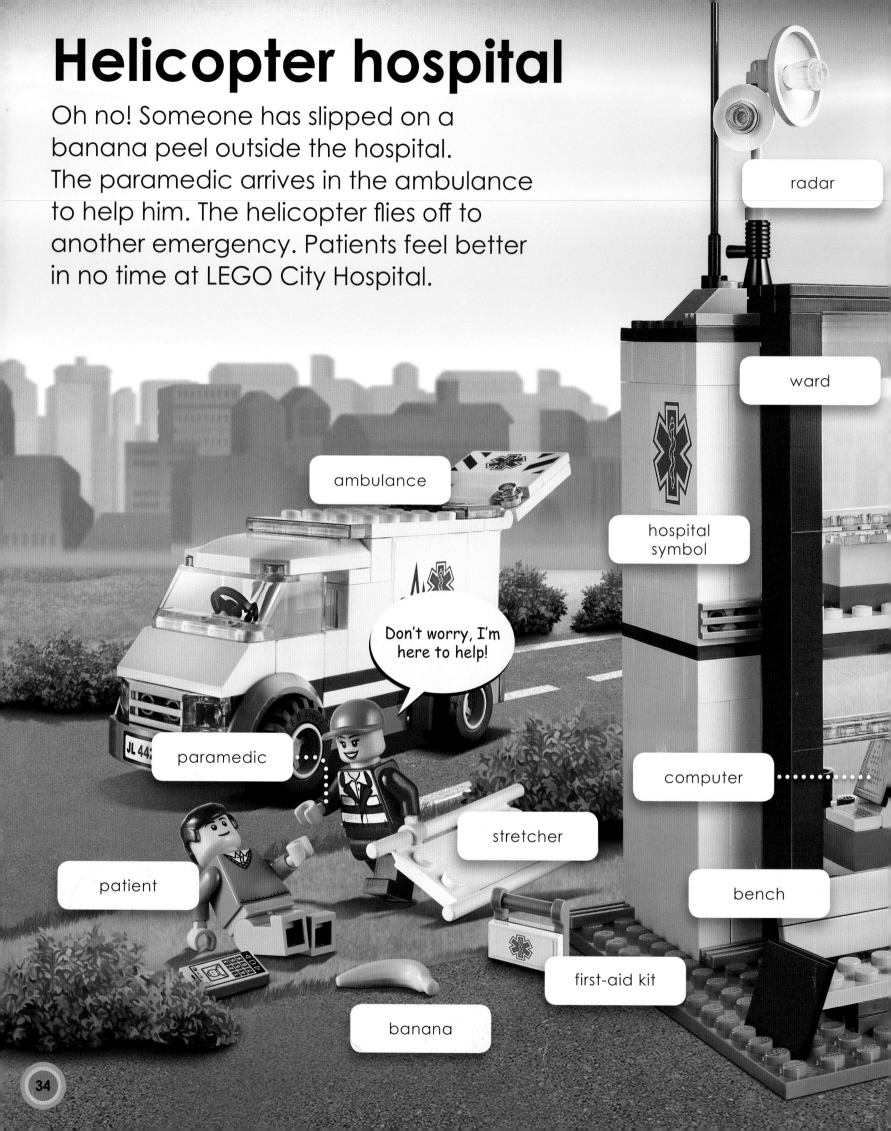

radar

ward

ambulance

hospital symbol

Don't worry, I'm here to help!

computer

paramedic

stretcher

patient

bench

first-aid kit

banana

# CHAPTER THREE
# On the Move

Lots of people live in LEGO® City. They use many different vehicles to get around. Some drive a car. Others take the bus or the train. For special journeys, people can fly in an aeroplane or board the ferry!

passenger

# At the station

Every day, trains begin and end journeys at LEGO City Station. Passengers wait for their train on the platform. They can buy a tasty hot dog if they are hungry.

roof

departure board

barrier

car

CITY CENTER 5min
AIRPORT 10min

LEGO

seating area

guard

taxi

TAXI

MS60050

passenger

taxi driver

# Heavy loads

LEGO City train yard is always busy. The crane is loading up the powerful cargo train. The train can pull trucks with vehicles on them. A mechanic checks that everything is running properly.

digger

bucket

flat wagon

bumper

tracks

Where's my cup of coffee?

mechanic

railing

train

60098

wrench

undercarriage

# Flying away

The aeroplane is ready for boarding. A baggage handler delivers the passengers' luggage. The post helicopter has just taken off. It has an important delivery to make!

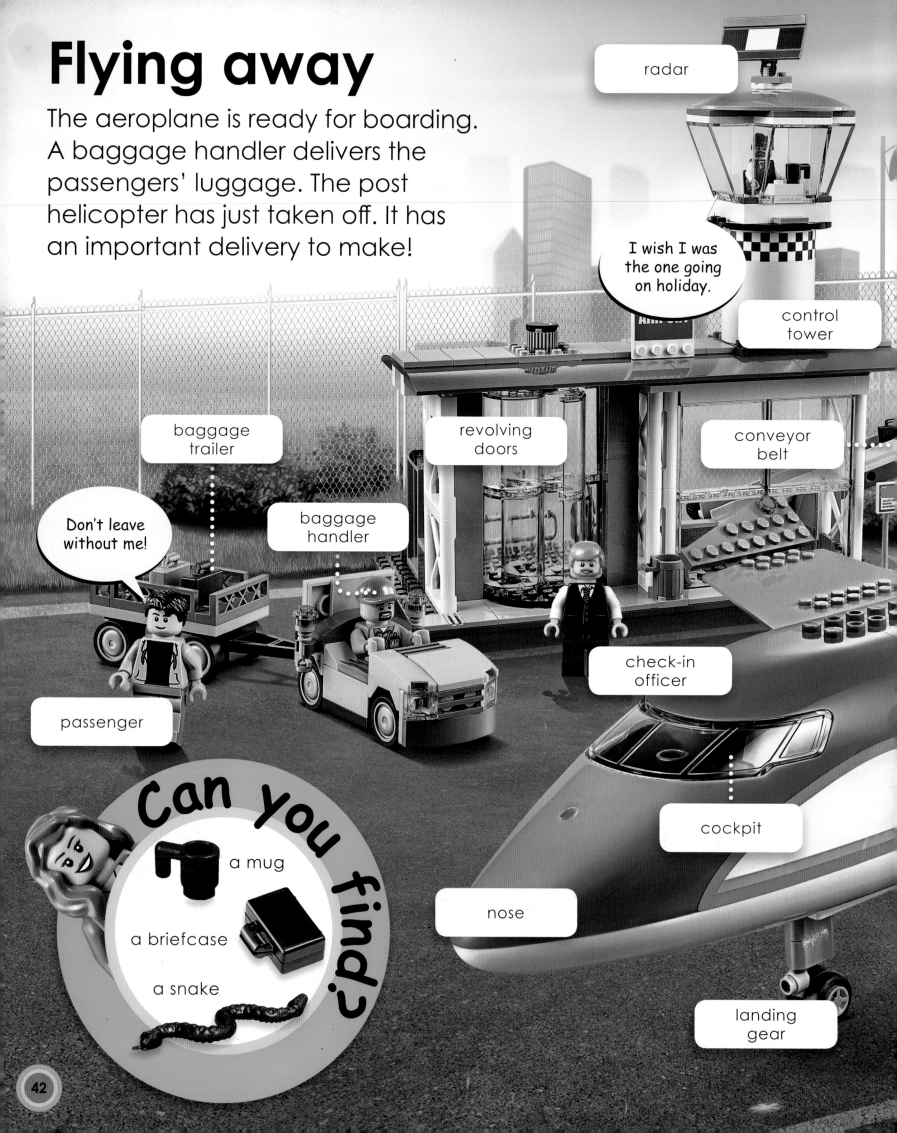

radar

I wish I was the one going on holiday.

control tower

baggage trailer

revolving doors

conveyor belt

Don't leave without me!

baggage handler

check-in officer

passenger

Can you find?

a mug

a briefcase

a snake

cockpit

nose

landing gear

pilot

post helicopter

stabiliser

fin

postbox

aeroplane

engine

postal worker

door

wing

pilot

hose

airstair

fuel trailer

# Air show

The LEGO City air show is happening today! Stunt planes fly high in the sky performing cool tricks. A mechanic fixes a biplane in the hangar. The biplane is nearly one hundred years old.

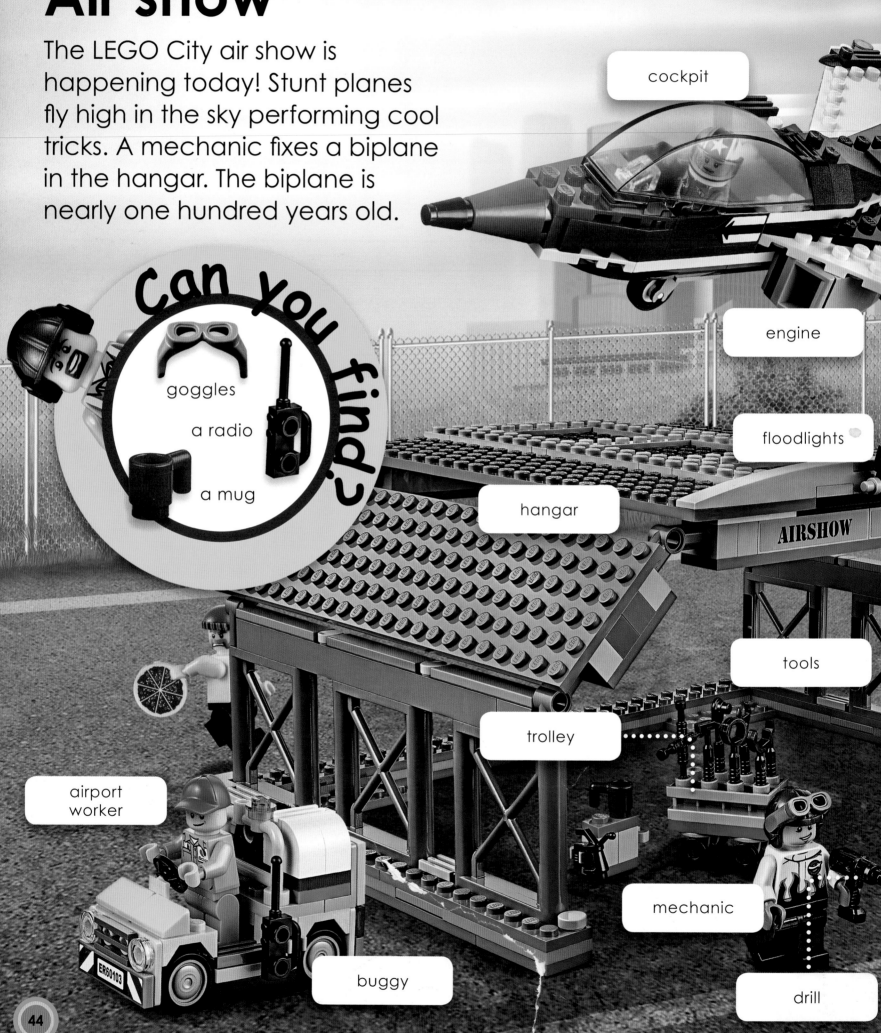

Can you find?

goggles

a radio

a mug

cockpit

engine

floodlights

hangar

AIRSHOW

tools

trolley

airport worker

mechanic

buggy

drill

# Race day

Engines are roaring, and dust is flying. It's race day at the LEGO City racetrack! Lots of different types of vehicles are racing. Drivers go as fast as they can. They all want to win first place!

portable toilet

Hey! Close the door!

service truck

monster truck

tyres

suspension

roll cage

buggy

engine

Eat my dust!

racing car

Can you find?

a red helmet

an 85 sign

a finish flag

truck

spare tyre

spoiler

stunt truck

Coming through!

4x4 off-roader

mudguards

headlights

rally car

air vents

dune buggy

windscreen

# Service station

The service station outside LEGO City is really useful. Drivers can fill up their cars with fuel or charge them with electricity. If their cars are dirty, they can take them through the car wash.

lamps

till

charge point

seating area

drinks

I choose pedal power!

pump attendant

car

bicycle

tow truck

# Let's go camping

LEGO City campsite is a peaceful place to stay. People sleep in cosy campers that have beds and kitchens inside. Lumberjacks collect fallen logs using their logging truck.

Can you find?

a map

a bone

a cat

motorhome

steering wheel

window

bear

bumper

life jacket

canoe

oar

lake

ER60057

# All aboard!

It's a beautiful day on the water.
The LEGO City ferry takes a car across
the bay. A sailor enjoys the waves.
A fisherwoman has just landed a catch!

radar

fishing rod

cockpit

fisherwoman

bridge

buoy

seat

car

driver

life buoy

ramp

# CHAPTER FOUR

# Beyond the City

Just outside LEGO® City a lot of different things are happening. Animals eat hay at the farm. Miners search for gold at the quarry. It is almost time for the astronauts to blast off in the space shuttle!

helmet

cockpit

launchpad

scientist

Help the police catch the pizza crook once and for all!

# On the farm

There is a busy farm just outside LEGO City. Cows and pigs live on the farm. There is also a grain field. The farmer lowers hay bales down from the big barn using a hook.

Who's that on the stable roof?

It's carrots for dinner tonight!

horse trailer

farm hand

exhaust pipe

trailer

tap

stable

pigsty

water trough

cow

fence

pigs

gate

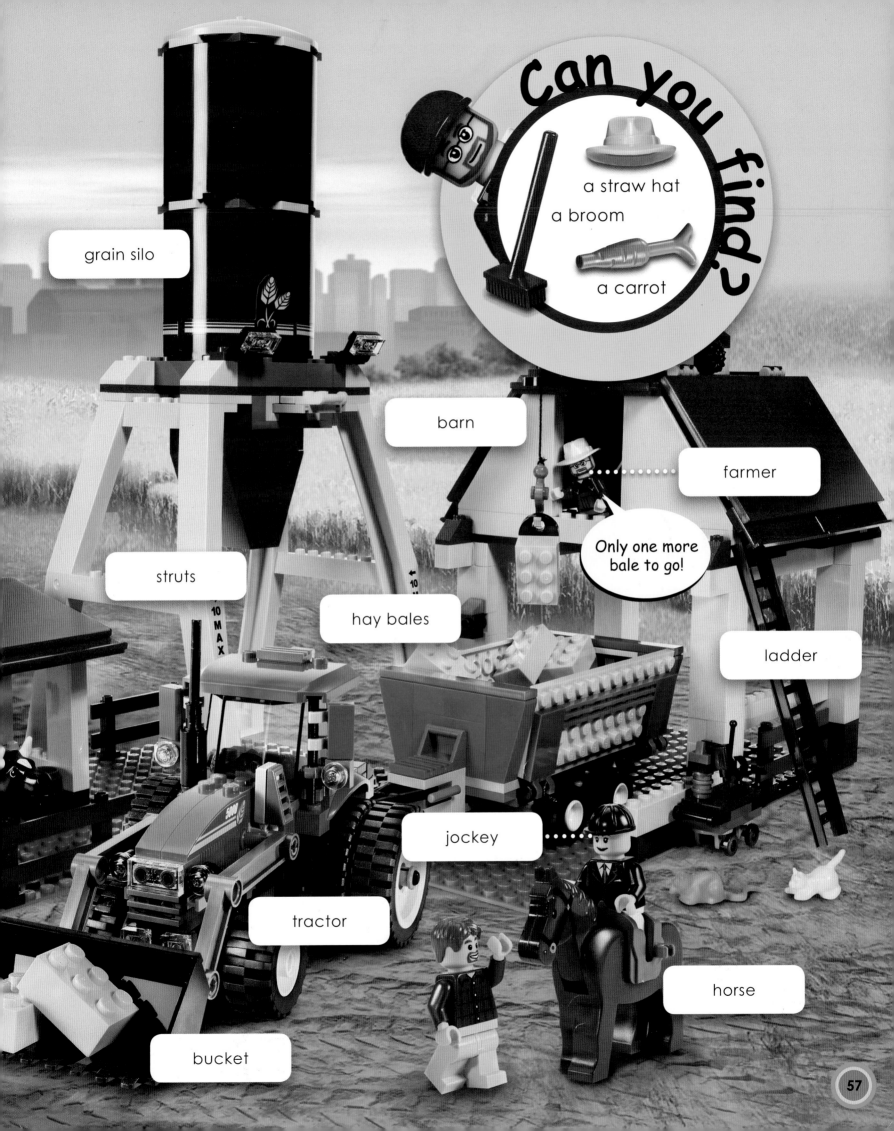

Can you find?

a straw hat
a broom
a carrot

grain silo

barn

farmer

Only one more bale to go!

struts

hay bales

ladder

jockey

tractor

horse

bucket

# Digging for jewels

The miners at the LEGO City mine are searching for valuable pieces of gold. They also mine rocks and put them in their big truck. Take cover before the dynamite explodes!

crane

controls

shelter

blast door

3...2...1–and a half...

SECURITY

explosion sign

HB 2846

train

pickaxe

boulder

miner

dynamite

rock drill

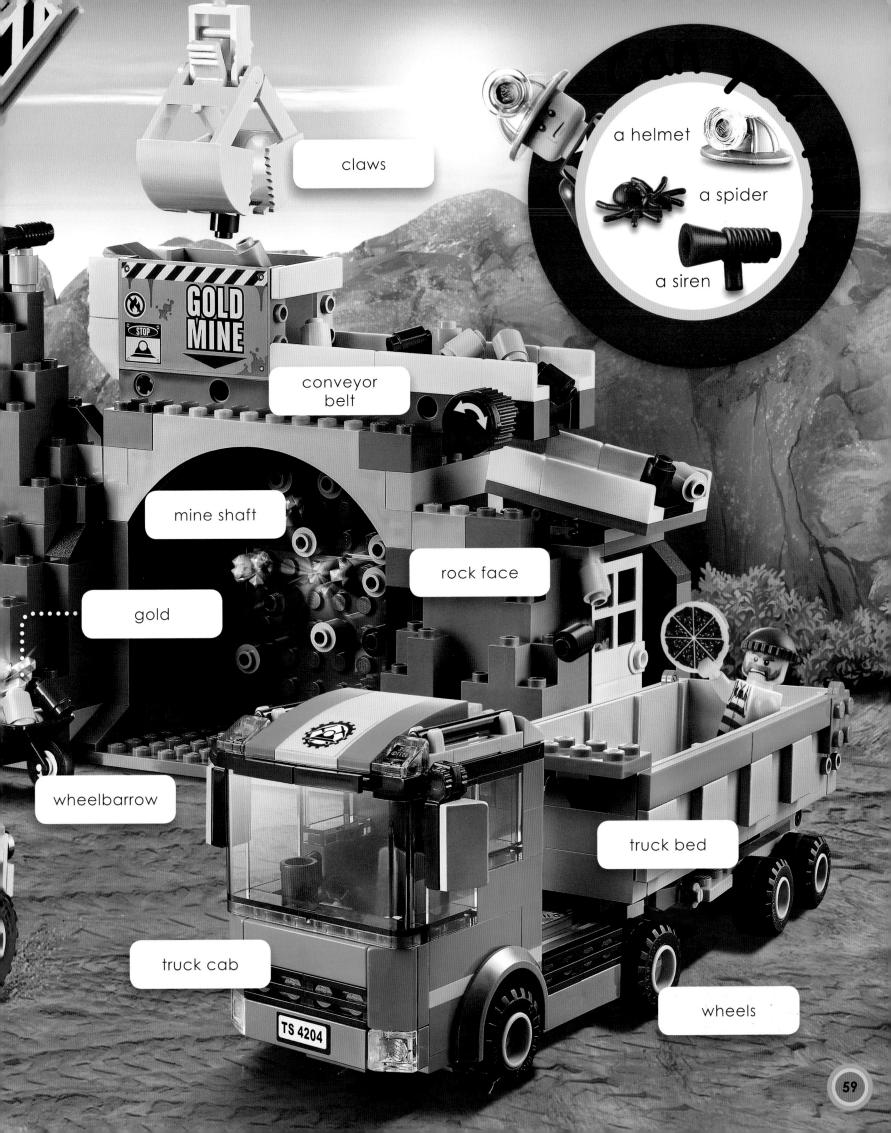

claws

a helmet

a spider

a siren

conveyor belt

mine shaft

rock face

gold

wheelbarrow

truck bed

truck cab

wheels

GOLD MINE

STOP

TS 4204

# Blast off!

It is launch day at LEGO City Spaceport! The shuttle will blast off once the astronauts are strapped in. Trainee astronauts learn how to use high-tech equipment at the lab.

moon

One small slice for man...

radar dish

jetpack

countdown

wing

camera

computer

scientist

moon buggy

lab

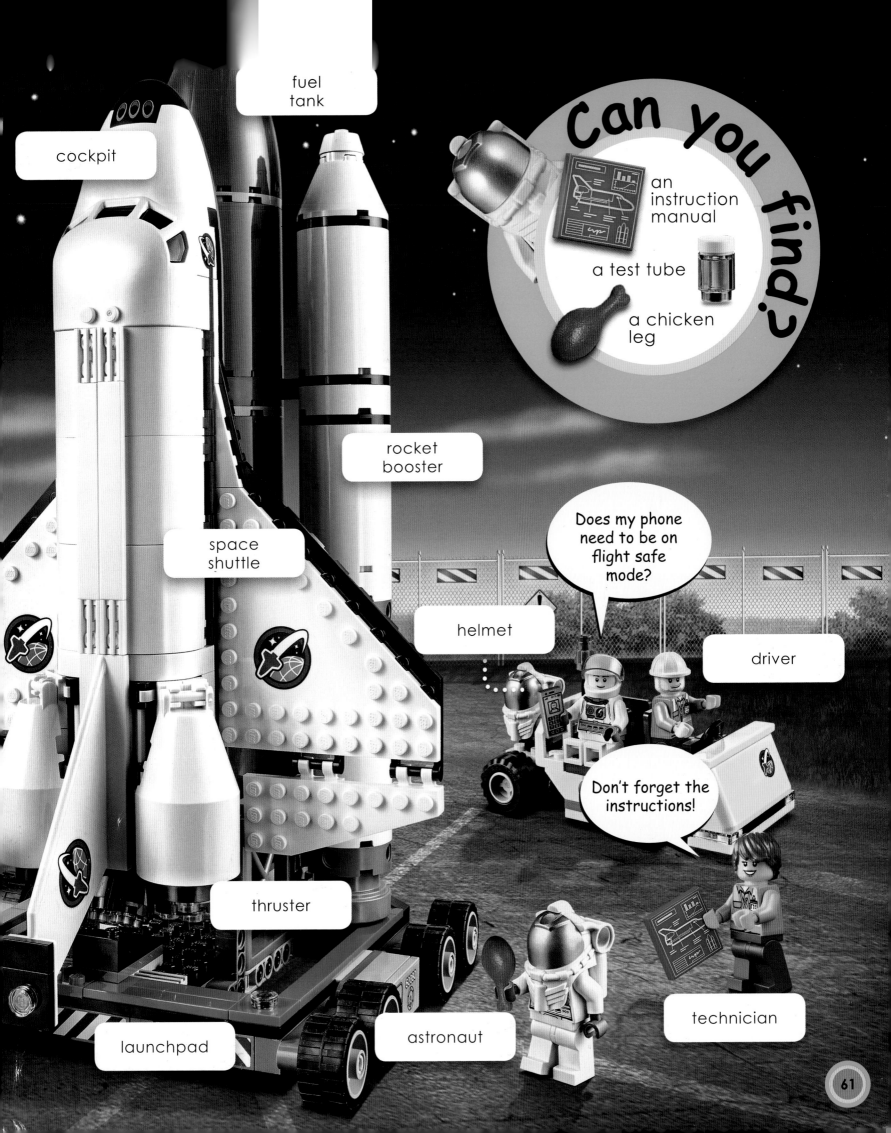

# Arctic base camp

A group of scientists from LEGO City are studying the ice. They have lots of research tools. One scientist is ice fishing. A polar bear has stolen his catch off the hook!

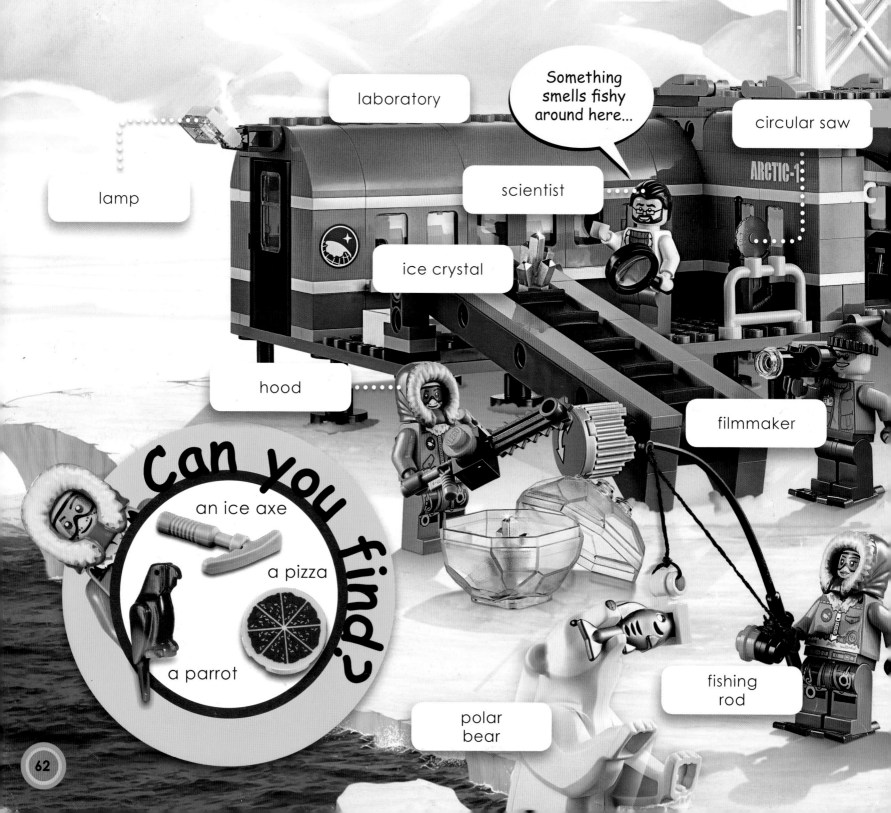

flag

laboratory

Something smells fishy around here...

circular saw

lamp

scientist

ice crystal

hood

filmmaker

Can you find?

an ice axe

a pizza

a parrot

fishing rod

polar bear

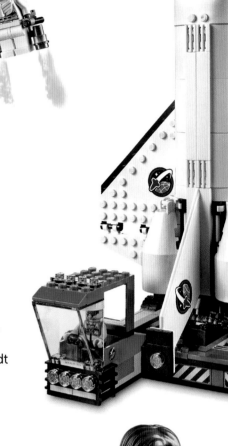

**Senior Editor** Victoria Taylor
**Editorial Assistant** Joseph Stewart
**Designer** Elena Jarmoskaite
**Pre-Production Producer** Kavita Varma
**Producer** Louise Minihane
**Managing Editor** Paula Regan
**Managing Art Editor** Jo Connor
**Publisher** Julie Ferris
**Art Director** Lisa Lanzarini
**Publishing Director** Simon Beecroft

**Reading Consultant** Maureen Fernandes

Dorling Kindersley would like to thank Lauren Adams, Jenny Edwards,
James McKeag and Rhys Thomas for design assistance, and Randi
Sørensen, Paul Hansford, Heidi K. Jensen and Martin Leighton Lindhardt
at the LEGO Group.

First published in Great Britain in 2018 by
Dorling Kindersley Limited
80 Strand, London, WC2R 0RL
A Penguin Random House Company

10 9 8 7 6 5 4 3 2 1
001-307133-Jan/2018

A CIP catalogue record for this book is available
from the British Library.

ISBN: 978-0-24131-007-6

Printed and bound in China

A WORLD OF IDEAS:
SEE ALL THERE IS TO KNOW

www.dk.com
www.LEGO.com

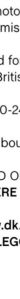